Praise for Nell Perry

"Nell Perry's poetry is a kind of etymological and bodily-oriented poetry which was deeply engrossing and felt expansive... Perry's work is work and sometimes a poetics of how meaning escapes and contorts us, of how social forces act upon the conceptions of the body and shift it under our own gaze can only be work, but it is bursting with avenues of exploration and a depth of image that is joy for the attendant reader."
Josh Allsop, *Osmosis*

Nell Perry's *Unspeakable Patterns of the House* is an organology of the psyche, the body, technology, the quantum realm and chloroplast, the habitat and the life-forms within it. [To read it] is to feel viscerally into the inherent polyphony and plastiglomerate matters of many agents and abstracted entities: the multivocal discourse of life and death in the anthropocene."
Maria Sledmere, *Blackbox Manifold*

"Nell Perry's poems return to sensation, argument, thought. I thought I knew what it was 'about' – a kind of kick against any vulgar logic of fate, from psychoanalysis to astrology to biology. But each time I read it something different happens, and what could be more pleasing: a living thing."
Luke Roberts

"Nell Perry's *Venusberg* is a deranged linguistic space; media language structures appropriated, disrupted and regurgitated as new and mutilated text. A fractured and psychotic incarnation of the gendered political machine, distorted into a polyphony of dismembered consumer-capitalist voices."
William Rowe

CREATION MYTHS

Nell Perry

Creation Myths by Nell Perry
First published in the United States by Filigree Press LLC
www.filigreepress.com

First Edition
ISBN: 978-1-971955-00-1

Cover Design: Open Air Design

CREATION MYTHS

Nell Perry

FILIGREE PRESS

For JPV

Contents

Creation Myth

in june we eat the silk of the housemother. we eat the scaffolding holding up the house. we eat the viceroy's public office. there is glue stuck to my pearly egg muscle. we turn our bellies to the yellow popsicle universe. the air is an aleatory music, a wet mass of bells. the pipes have voices like old walnuts. chrysalids hang like glands from the trees. the housemother's sinewy legs reach across the lawn like clumps of string. *in the isthmus of a sash window, the day is a tiny supplicant gesture of the hand.* the housemother's silk is torchlily red. she stoops on tiptoes like a columbary. the sky is a silver uvula. we eat the plush upholstery. we eat the doilies from inside bowls. we turn our middle intestines to the sky. we catch on the wind and float away.

Creation Myth

dogstar egg in the marrow flowers holds its thistle innards with baptismal hands, like the milky way swallowing its own shadow. the way an apple babies a moth, little poltergeist. the way that, through a bird's wing lens, you can turn a wolf into ligature, a cow into a quadrilateral. i have chewed ants into rubguts for a new kind of empathy, goodliest care shrubby with pink fungus. at the chancel arch, there is a gateau of glass. and over the spa town, orionids drop like blobs of butter. *nobody can stomach so literary an occurrence.* it is the most bankable thing that has happened since the last most bankable thing.

Creation Myth

errant egg if you live in a city. scold the egg its soap-bubble kidneys, no enamel in the road's chaotic pie-hole. it is raining little grownups. *it is raining a soup of everything in my balloon body.* livid little scud breathing opal caught in my mascara. adieu to the eggvault meat. boohoo to the bismuth atom froth like salmony lice, oyster green lice sticky on glass like an asteroid. dahlia splits cloud yolk into gelatine. au revoir day-old janes and claras and muckamucks swept into legwear. bon voyage mop squeezers. it is raining shrimp daughters. the world gushes out in zigzags.

Creation Myth

good morning egg is bite-me-billy blue. rolypoly peel-my-putty kind of blue to cake my eyes in the rot hole light of a mealworm moon. little shit shouty philips my beloveds do not let me be a tiny disgusted lever, air juicy caterpillar thick, celestial like a bauble. and being a ball of debris hearts is a hard kind of mutton fact i had wanted as medicine, a luscious layer. *i, the virginia peanut, rapunzelling my tongue bone through small holes and protocols.* learning i exist to spit the old moss and comets the errors the motley peach the yum yum out. elasticky a diamond jelly blockbusting my iris soggy blue as the blasphemous sky.

Interlude

uh oh here come the trash dads they do not believe in eggs they prefer more solid things like denim and the arctic. do not touch them they are a scuffle of light they are so sad they will burst right open, *oops they have unfolded all their gluten has fallen out.* trash dads stuffed full of winged horses and california rubies they are always splitting open do not worry about the trash dads they will be redeemed in the movie. they are so charming with their serrated mouths their massive disneyland mouths trash dads are really ok they just need to find the true meaning do not worry. they are always billowing open spilling out cherry stones but they will definitely realise the true meaning and they will be redeemed.

Creation Myth

desperately seeking an egg i am immediately inside of. where river is hosiery of a city all impulse and frills, a commerce of horseghosts with grasshopper heads. summer threads bluish glass tranquilly and isn't that terribly bijou. dilettante slosh in loosestrife and wee willy watery love-bomb just another kind of drown. frogbitten, even matted tentacles the dusty hairball i call my humdrum. you can't just think the flipside, little creep of a surgeonfish, you have to live it in your tripes your vesicles. i have hope for the milky sea ghosts the eel ghosts the gliding cloistral voids the cryptids. they will call you a needle-shaped interval of panic you cannot think outside of.

Creation Myth

carbon egg is a wolf bone a big woodsy egg bone a romeo so beautiful like a sticky millipede inside a drum. i feel very hollywood noir as if the melt of it is my evil twin a slime of galaxy to ooze heavy lilac out of your liver. *i kept my sticky on the inside i kept a slurry of vowels like an oracle.* a gutless egg lights up my whole body in the woods. it is an otherwise morning. i am late in every conceivable way except the one that means i am a membrane. i watch the egg become its own afterlife. sometimes my heart feels like a splayed arm but not on this liquidy morning that is otherwise. today it feels like the biggest eyelid ever to exist.

Interlude

if an heirloom washes up on the chew and pulp of the sea it is the archenemy of the egg. *no part of an egg is sour light boiled metal no part of an egg is beside itself.* if an heirloom takes place you cannot tell if you are a boy or a bile duct or an archduke or a lump of grey nothing. a million dead abdomens squid mouths whale vomit, hey just lay the night on me it's a sharp instrument, a squeaky clean. egg is a slowness and sometimes maybe full of flies but it is not an heirloom. ask the heirloom if you exist and you leave it up to the heirloom, never trust anything that has all the centuries in it.

Creation Myth

is there a work of an egg? night wraps its stupid texture around itself like a doughy tendon. the door of my room tries to tell me what blue doesn't mean and i am somehow always cringing in the corridor like a nowhere protein. the way that rooms can mean things at different times. and anyway the world arrives screwy as the pupil of a goat's eye and i guess that is how life happens. lip prints mauved to slick marble but a stripmall is sadder, sad as a manhour. and neon in the meat until we have walked ourselves bereft. *please don't one-up me to death, future self.* all i know is i want to be hot filthy fuchsia in the eclipse of a city's holy organs.

Interlude

pig egg, stag egg, earwig egg, guard them all inside your clotmouth, your lacklung. daisychain their frossylake skins into language. *i am a spew of tiny frogs.* i am speaking as a slimy hub. as a fondant eye. crush me big in the vocals huh in the glaciers. in the throat jelly. in the too large tongue. in the child of my slitmouth. the jewellery of my haemorrhage mouth. in the slushlake. hold their goblets their cockles their pebbly ancestries their spongecakey feelings hold them in your obvious mouth. this holding is called a grateful. i am speaking as an abrasion. as a mushy sac. as a frog nerve in a glass tube. i am speaking as the unmouth. the nothingmouth. the hole of the mouthfloor. hold the eggs cautious as they ache it is your one job.

Creation Myth

scythe of an egg in the water moult, holy as break-age. clouds crack their sugar yellow their trifle their chickenshit hearts, it is time to pry open the hem of my skeleton. to debouche, at this very cultish hour during which lungs happen. during which leg cake. *leg crystal.* rotten emeralds in the midges and margins. the river is theoretical an unsuspecting lip sewn shut. nymphy brains hair teeth make a middleman of the egg. it is an old larval skin pump kind of a year and the gullible organs just continue like nothing is different. one of these days we'll explode our bones right out of their dead constellations just you wait.

Interlude

imagine a pretty and inhospitable door in your body's cells and in your brain and in every building in every town. you would probably like to go inside the leathery glow the orangey homesickness. you would like to be part of its warm and luminous notions. so sorry satinette you are verboten. the door is not for you and nor is the ragged brick or the pristine countertop or the slithery porcelain. but it will eat you down to a stub and what a great honour that will be, pull back the glass and we're all just hanging there groundless and respectable like dishtowels.

Creation Myth

abyss egg a cathedral of glissandi, stones radiating cold embouchure, a tender edge. the click and strum of a train over the barricade is a long series of holes. there's light in the gutter like a soggy moon, it makes of us a small and ordinary gnawing. *always ask yourself, in the dark, whose pleasure is this, whose clarity*. whose glaciology garlands the tissues that stretch into voids. how might we swallow the horror of highfalutin ribs and voltas and oh boy their militant grace. feeling small is an art perfected by the thickness of walls, the clawed wood perfectly placed. on the other side the glorious nothing the everything of the world.

Creation Myth

cochlea of cement unegglike entangles slivers of a daily permute. in unbearable junctions, there are junk opals scalloping glass to the artery's rim, loving you brazenly. something about the daylight is insincere, like a tightfistedness. i have seen the brittle liberties of unmade bedding and wires shunt the morning out of its grimy tube so that it might breathe the sky down into its curved fingers. *some consolations are both small and life-saving.* the way hearts loosened from their timeline puddle in the underpass large and liquid. if i had a dream it would be to inhabit a purple that slowly evaporates, a neutrino sending shivers like a soft ballad out across the vanishing.

Interlude

what really gets you is the waxy mabels, opaque starry bodies shrivelled asterisms. how rotting heather clasps foetid glistening like a boreal hand. they have eaten into the dirt with rubbery tooth arrangements, they flail and undulate under the floorboards. bulbs of hair and mincemeat, faces drawn on with felt-tip. light clogged into morsel eyes spooky turquoise, a sour lick of clavicle holds the history and i have come apart again in the sediment. *bleary carbons, you are being too much.* this is the safe safe stuckness of the bog and i have cherished my mildew too hard the gristle said the skinful said, repulsive with clairvoyance.

Interlude

these are the watery eggless where do they end maybe in a wormhole or a soft blob. only eat all this terrible politics and afterwards here is a nice swamp for you a nice neighbourly a nice scrupulous but see this slimy muscle still flutters if we poke it, this is some living. please heave me up hollow space where a word was, i am obstinate blue like cold cathodes like low-grade romance. there is nebulous pulp in my openings, wool hair seaweed language in hard lumps, is this real i am tired of the gutting. if everything means everything else or maybe that's just incoherent light or the small vacancies that fluoresce in closed rooms.

Creation Myth

virid duchess egg for the meaty table flaked away like a metal. a burly ashy egg of winter oats and seeds and duck blood. rhombus of water is a threshold a belfry grieved by its overtures. did you dream a cattle-heart hole a pixeled louse a white moth on the ooid surface? *how curvature hurts.* swan bone, you know how to be in the world, what is this strip of correct light losing? in an old mill sluice's filthy foamy wisdom full of milk and botulism, petal gloss scums oily green. how we were already glittered with it, the river of our glassy cells.

Interlude

quiet please for the potato membranes they are very eligible they are eating your hard-boiled organs. deep in the february meat a slithery moon is leaking, nits of ice refract its slimy light. the membranes are a glutinous applique. glaucous sinews, filaments, oubliettes, my gushy citizen the hand that feeds you is a gummy weight a necrotic lump. the moon splits open spilling scribbly tinsel. *please be quiet it is bursting so privately it is bursting like a woeful egg.* the membranes prepare to digest, drawing together like a syrupy curtain. we are quiet now this is real synergy gluey like a proved fact like a flexed muscle.

Creation Myth

crocus a verb lustering at the day's throat yellow whirling prickly as a galaxy. bliss of screaming marguerites of gasping daisies. opal eye opens like blue chivalry i am laughing at my own joke towards which all patterns extend. some pearl blabbing feelers lilioid wastelands all memorial words batwing flimsy. *should i tessellate in the foxy brick, be less hexish?* it's sad but the day doesn't always love you back the body will distract you. it's ok, its just chaos pal, murky photons, old voltages, humanoid shapes in the grate.

Creation Myth

in may the sun is a radish a quarrel apple. ants harvest aphid milk, rose egg a jubilee of slubbed linen. wadded somewhere in the cliché, belle amour, gauche and incomprehensible. muon decay in the punchbowl. i am fathoming my wobbly head loose. interregnum as a sphere of starry giblets, an umbrella of ribs shabby and purple. *let it bead, typical hank, let it set.* our segments and how they line up uniformly. juliets crowding in with luxury amino acids and wax and their medallion eyes. lump mother shedding beetle flesh like petals.

Creation Myth

icarus egg a species of crochet that takes place inside of the eye. its trick is to rationalize the face until it is a clump of gel or a mealybug. this is one of the sadnesses that shine like a hyacinth: some days are like salesmen some days a special glue. i grow more eyes and wave them around but the flowers are desolate. we crawl out mollusky like yoga, my slivery body ten pieces of bread long. *maybe you can die of purple.* a majority of the eyeball for slow-floating jellies treacly vehicles elfins birdslick and shimmer daphnes, the full package. the cellar of the eye flew away on a bright giant exhale.

Creation Myth

inside a song nucleus, the bruise egg. a grieving of tree bones to wash a church greyer sopping. heart is not finished hothead: slip a thermal, shed a vortex, husk a throaty ocean. *glide a maple eyelid tiny swirling.* offices confect to galileo particles clotted energies quite suggestive. a jollied meat gloats for all the fredericks, the proper parts. so and so chiming in orbits and courtesies from the lindens the skylines hey jekyll and flotsam, please finesse us to bits. you make the world, debris, out of hand-me-downs seeds syllables afterglows, haunt in it like a grand piano.

Creation Myth

military hierarchy ate the sun egg spat up its curds elegant as a smooshed pear. earth presses buzzed lips into a turtleneck of gentles, dressy brassicas have a solidity low and hoarse. smooth feldgrau circumference a kind of clattering, my dairy chump whose liquidy gullet, whose glassy audacity. grabby asters pea flowers burnt bones are colleagues their pulpy phosphor a glittery kiss an aphrodisia. sun's milky souffle, breathy musculature a governing body and this instant a difficult trinket held chaotically. holy slippery eye full of dread and world and derision where i am both small and responsible. the sentences the blades the spines and garments fuss slovenly across the lawn like quiet dramas, condolences.

Interlude

from drain, from field's acidities, rot and glitter sung out of intestines, i have shrivelled my teeth. girl without a girl inside stepped onto the sea's luminous back, wind curving in lacquers that fleck the water densely. she raised from the sea a clavicle, said come on in the sea is clotted. *when i was a mother a beloved, the mother-of-pearl of my mother. when i was a mother a mammoth an ungulate.* little pierced thing alighted on thorn bone and the eggs hung onto the ocean. the eggs clattered to carbon. and we in the egg weep. and we in the egg mite, baby. how i love the yolk [i am afraid of the yolk]. the yolk of the yolk. we were in the water with weeds and laughter. the moon didn't notice its own ending. we dwelt inside of a cow. the moon said *get up idiot. there is more to learn from the insightful sky the perverted skin the doctrine of the stomach.*

Interlude

slurp of earth in the hogback pine, drivel of ridge to landmass your breath away. five o'clock is a bride, a sonnet of birch. we stomach the week alone as an oak, a slip of embedded wood. in the grass rut in the raking *it's all weird* all pulled to the hoop all burned to ash in a napkin. the forest is paranoid, goldilocksing. lump of eye, the word utters itself. and you are your own husband. i came to eat in the wasteglass, hefty follicle in the glitch of an oak. days got bitten, bake in the abdomen. bird is a resting place. dreg's light a spill of burnt neon.

Interlude

listening to sad boys cracking open their beautiful grievances. in lieu of a stringed instrument i haul a complicated wolf out of my chest. there is flood and some terrible fonts. raspberry cellophane fleshly sullen, a sprangling opera of deltoids. touches shunt claggy sequels, thin pieces of earworm. *how i let myself, beautiful intel, contain and expel.* a lopped object of gross geometry and irreparable softness and comfort tilted inwards. warlike in a body sank an opaque city, a permanence the vertebra made its own. there's work and there's work, know what i mean?

Creation Myth

it's enough to breathe through boiled cloth, watch doves fucking. limp flames curl unfussy burst corsages. *a cryptic egg folded in dead leaves i can see how charming its gravity.* enter the heart a clump of ditch lilies, washhouse bulbs, roadside night-nights, brassy diphthongs, bright blaring cynthias. busy boils down, gives you time for better things, like coral and cat-brushed pollen. how the delicate arch lures and shyly sulphurs.

how the sorbonnes the threads the legislatures engulf.

Creation Myth

exalt egg in a meadow, blunt chirring carapace and molar. sky is a puffball, a velocity. red soft shard in a cat's ear sparkles like dactyls. what it feels like to be tall dead stems after a plant dies. it is not possible to know everything. the sky is a housing estate. afternoon soon empties out as cashmere goo, small picture-wings to burn you with dozy gold longing. still i have lost things in the peaty silt smell of hydrangea smoke and vermouth. it is not possible to find them again. *it is not possible to know what the sky is.*

Creation Myth

egg as a rouged involvement. orange-tipped bobbies faint clean away on freckled lino, sleepy severed tongues. ivy gunk thickens glass, a dainty ceremony of winks, gussets, burgundy star spittle, portals so ballroomesque, pauses of sinister proportions. arms spread wide to mop promiscuous light withheld. *eat a love charm, eat a toad, eat a vitamin, eat a baby pony, eat a spirit guardian.* body horoscopes into the shape of a talon. beauty is a vulgarity doubled back on itself.

unfolding a universe blurted out.

Liminal

the physicists speak in short bursts, wring their wet towels, measure the thinness the length of my lagoon legs. they say, *will it flap?* say, *iconic muscles.* in the sky today, a colour like a splitting or the end of brightness. a colour of dead animals falling onto hard surfaces. i have such gorgeous veins but my brain is unexceptional, like papier-mâché or an ice-cream cone. i am an imprint on my own bones. i discovered the word *bird* in my room by the bedside, brushed it softly with my fingers. how the physicists say, *wishbone.* how they say, *cartilage.* i fold the words against my hip, imagine i am a rock garden.

Liminal

consider opening your mouth and swallowing the evolution of trees. trilobytes, glaciers, calcified lilies. i can no longer count on the water to corroborate my mauvy bloat, my heart like a hosepipe. since i have few acquaintances i buy a beer for some handsome bastard in the Lazarus bar, he has eyes like the morgue that spat me out. i can show you how to tilt your face free from your skull, how to swim collapsed, cleaned out, caved in, sans organs, cut en cabochon. i know what the sutures of an ammonite taste like, understand subtleties of ornament and slime. the difference between bone and bone and a wound and the abyss.

Liminal

many quirks to my name, i have told you and i have told you. howitzer body, evasive milky jaw, the loving mother that i was. how i swaddled a rock, fed it to my gullible husband. i'll grant you visibility if you wrap me in laurel and nurse me lightly in your palm. i dream about soft nubby insects in a sticky, uterine dark. you tell me stories you love about apertures, how things are implausibly sewn together. *it is only over thousands of years that speaking evolves into listening*. all the cuts you make like water's flinty, ululating breakage.

Liminal

make a slit big enough to skid from one sky to another. feel the infidelity of it, wake skittering with an urge to slash horizon. peel blueness back until you reach blueness again. there are similarities: a star's crystal chassis, its stringy radiolaria, untrustworthy moons. the deadline of a luring light's love. pelagic meats and rusted cardiac metals. how little collisions float like corrupted syllables. *clear wing, mirror wing,* as in: your body may not be legible. in the literature, in the icebox. nothing but a slender ellipse or a closed diamond or a biblical thud on the hull. flicker strangely to know you exist. any depth can be a kind of eating.

Liminal

refuse perfect circles so that something might always leak away. at night long swollen fingers stretch towards the rim of the moon's aimless jellyfish bell. my aquarist's prize, a ghost continent in the shape of a pulpy mouth, a celestial pancake. i roll pebbles in seagrass on the remnant of a ship's hollow gut, a gridlock of jagged symmetry. *anything wears down to soft-paste in agitated water.* sometimes i spit my own body out for the hell of it, outstrip red elegance, leave behind tendril skeletons in the dark like flowers made of dog's teeth. language of ragged openness folding in and out of itself momentously, as if the solid fact of me could hold back the ocean's voluptuous folds.

Creation Myth

wake up and holes can't hold anymore in. tread of ice weepy in carpet scruff, a bloom of velvet in the very long time ago. algal polygons adjust, creak apart in our gibberish fingers. *whatever impression is left, thin leavings bellying threads.* we swallowed down crevasses, their slimy conferences. old days rill at the edges like veal, the windows disgraced. softened quiet of a dulled lung. we swallowed crevasses that are sometimes entanglement, slick heaves soily in a wedge. we leaked endorphins from our whole hands, everything poured out slickly like a mirror.

Creation Myth

tiny slobbering suns, bloaty trails of meteor slop sleeping for us in the gob sky. palpate bony landmarks in the cloud fat secreted from sorry wetmeat. *damage is a holy pearl blood thing, debris visible through the dredge hole.* a flap of sky loosely dithering like manufacture. and laughter glitters up in gunky alphabets.

Creation Myth

boil the milky way, it is clogged with mothers. boil the milky wheat jelly. put a brooch beetle in the heart place made of desert stars and piss glass. *love me plastic in lobster flowers forever.* love me sisyphus in the grate cream, tumbling dark matter. you are a strange survival a festive opening. sung everyday astonished we dig the sun up to squeeze it's innards out.

Creation Myth

strobes of pulpy gender sliver in the wilding time. slits deeply oval so much oval. *you embody the pot and I, the paper.* I'll be the limb-wench and you'll be the brick-wife and the bees hook their feet to form a dangling parabola. there are snails screwed into the coal-ball earth. a scraped-out bowl of moon creeps from beespace in the fecal day sparkling. in the hen glow. a swag of hair in the moon horn. I will hold half the sea to my bullion ear. swollen bright bird in the foam a sad ruche. all things exchanged in the waste we make.

Creation Myth

no structure to realize egg as factory or plotline. there are limited ways to register what body absorbs, how it holds deferral, ruptures. people say the word *strangeness* over and over and its tiring. obsessed by a gulch eye embossed in the woodwormy strings of the bathroom floor. a carboned rose a pock of wood whited out. the crumpled mouth abrupt. there is a slice of wet light on the wall and cells unthread moussy where it shudders and breaks, worldless.

Creation Myth

being briefly vulnerable, i bled uncouth into the sauvignon. let me tell you how to hate a loved made thing for the life it feathers away. *come on now, with these feelings.* words as grey ladles and banal privacies thickening. and poems are not living, now laugh impulsively until you are sick. automaton egg's breached gilt wire halves hold a jewelled ego like a tiny carousel a dirty map. give me all your stupid thoughts and i will treasure them. all the things a conversation could have been oh such bad miracles.

Note on "Creation Myths"

These poems are a riddling work. They document two years in disarray; a chaotic almanac, a half-baked phenomenology experiment. The recurring image of the egg should not be understood as a concrete, real-world thing. In the 1980s Japanese TV drama *Saiyūki*, the character of Monkey was, as the song's opening song stated, 'born from an egg on a mountain top'. The egg motif in these poems may be understood on similar terms. At the same time as representing life, or perhaps potentiality, it also represents death, decay and regeneration.

Some of these poems have appeared in *A) Glimpse) Of): Experiencing the Radical Body*, edited by Dimitra Ioannou and Rebecca Wilcox; and *Litmus Magazine #5: the lichen issue*, edited by declan wiffen. Some of these poems were performed at the *Guillotine* reading series at The Beehive in Tottenham; many thanks to mjb.

Each poem is addressed to something or someone; these addressees include works of art, places, human persons, non-human persons (particularly those defying taxonomic forms of categorization, which I refer to, in the poem, as *liminals*), plants, inheritances, the notion of private property, practices of preservation, ways of being, ways of understanding, and times of the year. Some of these addressees, in no particular order, include Allen Fisher and Paige Mitchell; the river Stour; Louise Bourgeois; Stodmarsh nature reserve; my father Douglas Perry; bluetits and sparrows; the shaggy ink cap; Montparnasse, Paris; dragonflies; Museum Willet-Holthuysen in Amsterdam; Adrián Villar Rojas' exhibition *Poems for Earthlings*; bog bodies; inflatable skydancing tube persons; the swan under the causeway; the robin in the underpass; campus lichen; my gender non-conforming colleagues and students at Kent; the much-mourned rose tree; *The Kalevala*; the Church of St Martin cemetery; the common blue butterfly; the comma butterfly; the orange lily; the blackbird with one tailfeather (a.k.a 'Scraps'); the wood pigeon from the Pound Lane car park; the grasses in the meadow between Harbledown and St Dunstans; the archaeopteryx; the coelacanth; the platypus; the sailfin; coral; mallards; and the winter dark. Thanks, and love, to all.

Imaginary Deaths

A small tragedy of the everyday: in the garden, a woodpigeon mauled by a neighbour's cat. 6am, and you wake me with the formal, childlike sadness. You are especially vulnerable to animal pain. Clumsy with sleep, I approach the situation like a blunt object. The morning air is brisk and gauzy yellow. The cat has dragged the pigeon across the lawn and onto brick and moss underneath shaggy bamboo where it shivers, one wing fanned flat, the other tucked such that it appears, at first glance, missing. A blizzard of straggled, slate-tipped feathers trails across the grass, their soft white edges flickering gently in the wind.

Having presumed it dead, you have improvised an armoury for the disposal of its little grey body, but its rose-grey chest is still rising in tiny bursts. Neither one of us has the stomach to kill it, nor any sense of how to go about it if we did and I can tell there is some silt or sediment of shame stirred up in you from growing up a boy, because men are meant to decide the best time for things to die, to roll up their sleeves and get it done. The pigeon's suffering, its pain is so ugly, but our inadequacy is uglier. We pick up the feathers one by one and wait for it to die.

I try to make a connection by looking into its blank and glassy eye but all I imagine is its deep disappointment. In my head I tell it I am sorry and that it is not alone. I search memory for words of kindness or solace but find only the Lord's prayer with some lines muddled or missing. It feels dusty and broken as I recite it in my head. You suggest covering the pigeon with a cardboard box so that it might recover from its shock quietly and without threat, but when we approach, it stands up and staggers under the lemon balm out of reach.

Later, it clashes about on the kitchen windowsill, raises a flurry under the box hedge. Finally, it settles blinking and sphinx-like on some raised brick by the wooden shed. We move around the garden slowly and quietly like wraiths. I watch it from the corner of my eye, half expecting it to explode in a mess of pain and panic and feathers, the oozy corners of life's fragile envelope spilling its death and reality. I imagine what I must look like to the pigeon, a vast and unpredictable shape. I read somewhere that pigeons have the cognitive faculties required for reading language. The sun is oppressively hot so I drag my chair into the cool comfort of the wisteria's pooling shadow. The pigeon sits like a ragged sentinel on its brick plinth, rising onto pink feet to fend off the harassment of flies. I wonder how much the pigeon is dying; whether it is dying more or less than the rest of us, or whether there is no difference at all since you can't precisely quantify how much something is dying. I am always wondering whether I am dying the correct amount.

By five, the garden is thick with fronds of shadow. We leave the pigeon shored up against a narrow crevice between the shed and a part of the fence curtained by next door's pendulous grapevine. You tell me that a bird's neurons are smaller and closer together, which means they can think faster than humans. We are both deeply haunted by our uselessness. By the evening, the pigeon has alighted on another neighbour's back fence. Perhaps tired by the effort, it sits huddled and sad. There is something epic about it, like an old sea captain raging on a rainy cliff edge.

My latest imagination of death is as a continuum of choices interrupted by small intervals of living. Floating wisps of ethereal light investing themselves like long cords of string. It's rudimentary; too linear; but I like it fine for now. Floating and choosing. I tell you I think about death too much. *How much is too much,* you ask. Pretty much all of the time. So much that it inflects everything. You say that it is probably normal, that most people do it but they're not really aware of it. This makes me feel better because it plays into my fantasy of being special and smarter than everyone else, which in turn is a bottomless fear that I am actually very stupid.

After my Dad died I had an imagination of death as a giant egg towards which we are all slithering inching thinking ourselves in the thick of things. Nice, you know, but kind of twee, a little like Gandalf talking about death as the 'next great adventure.' I like the idea of death as a beginning rather than an ending; I guess we all do. I am nonetheless sure we misunderstand eggs and their potentiality. Ourobourotic, amniotic.

Lately I have been thinking about the possibility that we have each already died many times. Not in a reincarnation kind of a way, but within our own lifetimes. I have to separate this from my compulsive habit of imagining more danger than there is in any given situation. Like when a lorry speeds past your pedestrian body and you imagine having reached an arm out at just the wrong time and what the reality of that ugly cleavage might look and feel like, the shock of it. What I'm thinking about is more like the multiverse, a cascade of possibilities where one self dies and splits off like a twig bent too far away from the stem while the stem continues upward splitting more as it goes. I can't help thinking about the terminal point because what happens then? At other times, I imagine the multiverse as an endless layer of ever-expanding realities beginning at the quantum level and up through microbia, gut flora, anthills, rabbit warrens, human cities, solar systems, galaxies further and further upwards until you reach the quantum level again. A bit like saying what if the universe is a ball of lint in god's bellybutton or what if the world is god's marble glass eye and why is it so hard to believe fully in any of these versions, sometimes they just go round and round in a dizzying loop.

I am too hot in the sun. It is the hottest day of the year so far on record and obviously the planet is dying. When I was in my teens and twenties I had a weird habit of telling people I wouldn't make it to thirty, to forty, to fifty and so on, and I believed it and lived accordingly or perhaps unconsciously trying to fulfil my own prophecy such that by a neat trick of idiocy I would have made myself a teller of my own retrospective fortune. I am forty this year and every day I wonder how much longer as if, like a cosmic punishment, I have come to believe my own adolescent bullshit. I am in the hot garden and I notice a smear of grey-brown on the page of my book where a fly has been crushed by a careless finger. Sometimes it feels like death is everywhere and how can you not think about it all the time?

When it viscerally and concretely occurred to me that I could die at any moment I was in my living room and I imagined the ceiling caving in, not just once but as a succession of possible collapses. It is funny to me that this particular imaginary death hit me, as they say, like a ton of bricks. I imagine myself alive and pinned bleeding crushed in the rubble for hours, days. I really know how to escalate an imaginary death.

All the possible ways I might have already died: jumping from one brick wall to collide with the sharp corner of another; removing another small death from within; the state's intrusion into the body at multiple intervals; the grafting of skin onto skin; a plurality of strange houses and passenger seats of cars; a Greek hostel's rain slicked tile; feral cocktails, toxic fizzing; smashed glass; foliage draped across a stop sign; careless haste; an open manhole; a national express bus. I have considered the possibility that I am already dead, but it is perhaps the least convincing imaginary death because it is so plausible.

I do think it would be something to move excitedly towards death rather than endlessly unconsciously trying to keep it at bay. What if we could embrace it with anticipation, angle ourselves towards it the way roses turn their heavy silky heads towards the sun? After my Dad died, we bought a plaque to be installed at the crematorium where his ashes were scattered around a tall and shadow-pocketed pine. It read, *now I know something you don't know.*

It cannot simply be a question of zero-sum transferral. We can't think outside of quantity. The whole 21 grams thing. We imagine heaven as a continuation of earth except everything is perfect, but what would stop us from ruining paradise in the same way we are ruining earth? Nothing, of course, and obviously 'heaven' is just a means of making people accept the horrible circumstances of their lives; a way of saying hey, don't fuss it'll be your turn next time, next time around.

The pigeon made it as far as the car park behind our garden fence and it was still there the following day crouched beside a wheelie bin looking ruffled and sad. We brought it seeds and scattered them on the barren tarmac, but we scared it into the shadows. We are humbled by our spectacular inability to help it, our naivety. The alley between the Victorian terraces is strewn with red rose petals like the remnants of a festival. Sometimes being alive is inexplicably hard and excrutiatingly beautiful.

Death is held cheaply because it has an excess of meaning which is to say it has no meaning, or rather that its various meanings cancel one another out. Conceived of as a pure and final end it is a voluptuous nothing. If we cannot abide or comprehend uncertainty, we petulantly refuse all other possibilities. Or we suffer from a great failure of the imagination. To extend what is beyond its own parameters is just the ego unable to comprehend beyond itself. Ego vs egg: the great existential face-off. I dream of something more flamboyant, less stark and arbitrary. Not comprehensible per se, but strange and epic. And this is the fallacy of wanting to know the great cosmic plan when there is no plan, no system, no order just meaty glassy carbon chaotic and ridiculous. The annexation of death from life makes it creep solemnly slyly like a viscous delusion, always there and not quite there at once and breaking through the surface in weird and disastrous ways.

I carry this thinking around like a shabby filthy circus, a feathery dribbling carnival, a Dickensian necklace of bones and teeth. I'd like to shear it clean off, to cut loose and float lightly from its swampy seaweedy notions.

The fetishization of the dead in all aspects of the quotidian is called history. We close a life down when it ends and make a neatly wrapped story, a cleanly cut stone thing. What if a life is not a singular and separate entity? What if our consciousnesses overlap and bleed into one another even as we live and die? Not figuratively, I mean, but literally. Like a pooling of subjectivities. I, then, would be I but also you he she we though the I might only be able to see one side of it like the facet of a huge and luminous diamond. I would be both responsible and not responsible for my own self's river of listening, a city of selves making and unmaking, learning and unlearning. This is a difficult imaginary death, we are so accustomed to our walled off bodies, our tight little projects of self.

The gothic romance of graveyards, crematoria, sanctuary pockets within urban and suburban sprawl. Often, we think of death as having a contaminant quality. Morgues, mortuaries, mausoleums, crypts, cata-combs are spaces of horror; undertakers are imagined as gaunt, their work suits, strangely archaic top hats and frock coats. People who think about death a lot are labelled morbid, ghoulish, unwholesome. We worry that if we get too close to death, if we spend too much time looking at it, it will fix us with its ravenous eye, or seep into our open pores. And yet, we are obsessed with it, intrigued by its iconography, drawn to watching it on screen, fascinated by its strangeness, its terror lurking tantalisingly behind a velvet curtain, or unthinkingly revelling in its sanitized and pre-packaged tropes: skulls, skeletons, persephonic tableaux, Opheliana, gothic narratives, murder mysteries, ghosts, mythic and symbolic voids, underworlds, zombies, vampires. As if we can look at it only sideways, askance, peripherally, because to look at it head on is to invite it in.

Why is life a sequence of endings? Why choose to imagine yourself dying every moment? It doesn't have to be this bleak, I'm telling you. Who said happiness was the opposite of death? Who spun these desperate yarns that thread through all our stories? I am tired of death as the anvil the trapdoor the open jaw. I want death as a kaleidoscope a cascade a confluence of rivers a clattering of wings. I want death as a rushing in of air. I want to burst from my body like a glitterbomb. I am tired of these small and sad ideas. I want a rich and melodic eschatology full of never-before-imagined colours and musical notes. I want a wide and expansive horizon. I want to stop sentimentalizing death and fearing it and annexing it into shadows and dirt. I want it to be shiny and brilliant like a turquoise marble. I want to take away its stiff pageantries, its cold and prim greys. I want its uncertainty to be glorious and seething with possibility. I demand a new kind of death.

Fuck notions of time as an hourglass as currency as a long brittle rectangle. Fuck the battle music, the dreary organs, the lip syncing of puritanical dirges. The happiness-industrial-complex, the neoliberal folk myths and markets, the toothless elegies, the sad endings and dehumanizations. The hierarchies of grief, the watery obituaries. The lathery narrativizing. I will imagine a new death airy and operatic and sparkling like a wayward particle.

Maybe if we were not conditioned to understand ourselves our social relations in terms entirely structured around possession and ownership. If we did not play these fort-da games. If we did not make a house from these languishing symbols. If we weren't born so helpless and gullible. If we weren't so afraid of our bodies' edges. If we could learn from the bats the flying fish the lizards the dappled owls the whales. If we didn't always imagine ourselves as the sun. If we weren't so seduced by sequences. If we had any real sense of scale and proportion. If the stories we told were not so full of closures, inevitabilities. I will tell a story so open the world will fall in and turn inside-out. I will tell a story as open as the sky. I will tell stories like oceans and galaxies. Vast, soupy, impure stories. Dreamy, joyful, entangled stories. They will have no edges and endings. They will have no margins, but spill and rush off the page like waterfalls.

Aesthetic of death: pine needles, heavy perfume, grey polyester. Sticky rain. Gravel. Elaborate cursive. Not having any real sense of how things are made. The illusion of wrong choices. Overture from a bad eighties movie with colonial sentiments. The sense of your precarious teeth. An emotionless education.

www.ingramcontent.com/pod-product-compliance
Lightning Source LLC
Chambersburg PA
CBHW040227130726
48054CB00028B/263

* 9 7 8 1 9 7 1 9 5 5 0 0 1 *